THE BLESSING ZONE

"The Power & Significance of His Presence"

By Dr. Victoria E. Jones

Publisher: Victorious Women Ministries
© 2014 by Dr. Victoria E. Jones

All rights reserved, including the right to reproduce this book or portion thereof in any form whatsoever.

This book is published by Victorious Women Ministries, which is located in the United States of America. It is protected by the United States Copyright Act, all applicable state laws, and international Copyright laws.

Publisher: Victorious Women Ministries
www.victoriouswomenmin.org

For more information regarding special discounts for bulk purchases, please contact
www.victoriouswomenmin.org

Scripture quotations marked NKJV are taken from *The Woman's Study Bible, New King James Version*, copyright © 1995, by Thomas Nelson Publishers in Nashville, Tennessee.

Scripture quotations marked NIV are taken from *The Comparative Study Bible, New International Version,* copyright © 1984 by Zondervan Publishing House in Grand Rapids, Michigan.

(ISBN 13) 978-0692319451
(ISBN 10) 069231945X

Library of Congress Control Number: 2014919332

*Dr. Victoria E. Jones dedicates this book
to all who hunger to experience
"The Blessing Zone"*

Wishing you success!

Acknowledgements

There are several people who have honored me with their professional skills and capabilities as this writing journey unfolded. I must acknowledge their contributions. Many have contributed in tangible ways, and others have been there to support me and encourage me to keep going. Truly, I am grateful for this moment in time; as I know that, without divine intervention and the advocacy of many, this writing would be incomplete. The team of editors includes Tenita Johnson, Diane Poupore, Connie Drake Wilson, and Christine D'Angela. I am indeed honored by your outstanding work, spiritual insights, and wisdom. I am grateful to Diane Poupore for an extraordinary labor of love through the arduous editing process. I am grateful for her servant's heart. In addition, thank you to Connie Drake Wilson for allowing God to use her to ignite a spark in me to complete the book. I want to extend a special thank you to Michelle Malinowski for her expertise, problem solving skills, and patience in finalizing *The Blessing Zone*. I am grateful for her commitment to excellence. Thank you so much!

Those who have supported Victorious Women Ministries over the years have been an encouragement. With the many donations offered to the ministry, several families have been blessed. The ministry has stimulated me to go further, to reach beyond the impossible, and to discover that through service to others, I have encountered my personal blessing zone in magnificent ways. I am thankful for donors who have blessed hundreds of families. I trust God to show His divine favor upon your lives.

I desire to acknowledge Pastors Larry and Linda Smith of New St. Mark Baptist Church, Detroit, Michigan, for trusting me to lead the first Victorious Women's Conference event. Your confidence in me ignited a compelling vision for me to move forward with a ministry that would have a strong focus on women and families. My own childhood laid a foundation for the ministry, and the work at New St. Mark served as a catalyst to birth Victorious Women. I am grateful and thankful for you.

North Ridge Community Church, Cave Creek, Arizona, under the leadership of Pastor Mike Burnidge, is also acknowledged for his instrumental role in this writing. It was the Women's Ministry – In Touch Fellowship – that allowed me to first tell the story of my experience in Shanghai, China. Bettie Goodman invited me to share my testimony. This opportunity opened the door to discuss the journey to my personal blessing zone through its unconventional route. I am so grateful and thankful for North Ridge.

Family encouragement has played a significant role in this writing. My great thanks are extended to my husband, daughter and son-in-law, and my grandson. My Lord and Savior Jesus Christ has truly been an encouragement that has allowed me to repeatedly soar to my blessing zone. He is the center of the convergence of His plan, my plan, and my desires. Every day I am grateful to God for honoring me with His presence and the profound experiences in my blessing zone.

Table of Contents

Acknowledgements

Foreword

Preface

Chapter 1: Discover Your Blessing Zone!.. 5

Chapter 2: Enrich Your Life......................... 19

Chapter 3: Explore God's Plan.................... 27

Chapter 4: Engage with God....................... 37

Chapter 5: Experience the Richness of the Blessing Zone 45

Chapter 6: Enhance Your Relationship with Him 57

Chapter 7: Expand Your Vision to See Your Blessing Zone 75

Appendix 85
Study Guide
Points to Remember

Foreword

Don't block your blessings -- you may have heard those words before. In her book, *The Blessing Zone*, Dr. Victoria E. Jones gives a fresh perspective by laying out a blueprint for experiencing God's plan to the fullest extent for your blessed life. The author masterfully brings the reader into the realization that there is, in fact, "a place to bask in the presence of the Lord: a place of refuge, peace, and fullness." You will leave this intimate reading experience feeling like the participants when they leave Victoria's workshops: with a renewed, transformed, deepened relationship with the Lord. Can you envision a more enriched life for yourself? It's time to reap the benefits of discovering and enjoying your blessing zone!

As one of Victoria's professional associates and personal friend, I have experienced a more enhanced, intimate relationship with God through her teachings, writings, and personal conversations. Professionally, Victoria has significant experience in leading and facilitating conferences, workshops, and retreats aimed at developing spiritual and professional growth for all individuals, no matter where they are on life's journey. It is through these types of unique encounters with the author that people are able to realize that God has a master plan for each of us. Each one of us can know what that plan is if we only connect, listen, pray, and receive God's customized, personalized benefits from our own blessing zone!

This is no ordinary "how-to" book! *The Blessing Zone* is timeless. You can read it now and discover months and even years later that Victoria's blueprint on how to engage with God and explore His plan for your life is still relevant, contemporary, beneficial, and in line with God's Word. God's plan for you is just for *you*! Victoria shows you how to access your individualized plan. The journey to your blessing zone may take time, but you will get there. It is through the pearls of wisdom, so eloquently examined in this book, that you realize that the blessing zone is for real!

In order to properly access your blessing zone, you must put on your spiritual lenses and open your mind and heart so that your pathway is clear, your vision is sharp, and you are ready to travel to a place where God is forever present. You will discover a place full of joy, peace, comfort, and love! *So God created man in His own image; in the image of God He created him; male and female He created them. Then God blessed them, and God said to them, "Be fruitful and multiply; fill the earth and subdue it; have dominion over the fish of the sea, over the birds of the air, and over every living thing that moves on the earth."* (Genesis 1:27–28 NKJV). We were created to be blessed. Don't block the blessings!

Through Jesus' blood that He shed on Cavalry's cross, the effects of sin have been removed so we can once again live in the fullness of God.

Because He died and rose again, we can live and enjoy our promised inheritance, as further explained in *The Blessing Zone*!

By: Connie Drake Wilson

Preface
The Blessing Zone
A Match Made in Heaven

Early in life, my mother instilled in me a strong sense of responsibility and service to others. My mother was a role model for helping people. She did this out of her very meager means. I learned from my mother how to do much with very little. For years, we had meals of beans and cornbread six days a week, and on Sundays, my mother added chicken to the meals. Sundays were always special. If a neighbor wanted to join us, my mother taught us to take less so that others might enjoy Sunday dinner with us. We learned to do this with a grateful heart. In reflecting back, this was the best weight management approach I have ever experienced!

Learning to serve others at an early age clearly laid the foundation for realizing the power of service and the pathway to exceptional experiences in what I call, "The Blessing Zone." My brother, Bill, and I would search neighborhood streets for soda bottles, which were worth pennies. Bill and I would find bottles which may have been tossed into the street by party goers, and it served as a revenue stream for us. Bill never said no when I proposed that we hunt for bottles. I was the captain of this sister/brother partnership and always shared the revenue with Bill as well as my mother. My younger sister, Portia, would wait patiently for our return as we would remember to bring her a grape gumball from our profits. We were all grateful for the abundance provided by the Lord through this innovative approach for building a revenue stream. Little did we know at the time, this practice also helped with removing unsightly litter from the neighbor streets located on the lower eastside of Detroit.

The revenue sharing process provided a means for serving others. I would collect the pennies over the course of a year. When my mother needed assistance with purchasing food for the household, I learned to support her. It was such a joy to have this type of responsibility to help my family. God showed me at a very early age the joy of giving. It was a tremendous setup for discovering the power of the blessing zone through service to others.

My strong desire was to serve others. Service created an overwhelming feeling of positive impact. I was on my journey of discovering the Lord. At that point in my young life, I did not know Him, although I knew of Him through times when my mother listened to her spiritual hour on the radio. I found myself wanting to know more about Jesus Who served as the center of so many songs and sermons on the radio. Program after program spoke of Jesus, and it was intriguing to me that there was so much attention on developing a relationship with Him.

We were not a church-going family. My mother told of her stories of getting to know Jesus. She proudly reported that she was baptized at New Salem Baptist Church in Detroit, Michigan, at the age of 11. Mother shared how she would walk to church every Sunday with neighborhood kids, and as she told us the story of her church encounters, my mother would beam. I thought to myself, I sure wish I could go to church and gain the beautiful beam that my mother has. The encounter of my initial blessing zone was unfolding.

The hope is that in reading *The Blessing Zone*, you will unlock the power of the presence of the Lord through service to others. You will see the juncture of God's plan, your plan, and your desires. It will be a transforming experience as you encounter your blessing zone. May the blessings of the Lord be yours now and forever.

THE BLESSING ZONE

Chapter 1: Discover Your Blessing Zone!

Busyness seems to define us these days. Between multitasking, juggling appointments, demanding bosses, challenging customers, and unrealistic coworkers, it seems that there is no time to pause and acknowledge the presence of the Lord in our lives. Through our multitasking and scheduling, our forecasting, and our planning, where does He fit in? I searched to gain insight on whether or not there is truly a blessing zone – a place to bask in the presence of the Lord: a place of refuge, peace, and fullness.

The Word of God tells us, *Never will I leave you; never will I forsake you* (Hebrews

13:5 NIV). God is wherever we are. No matter what we are doing, He is there. In the midst of our multitasking, He is there. In the midst of juggling appointments, He is there. In the center of demanding bosses, God is there. Even when we're serving those challenging customers who constantly remind us of their expectations – you know the ones I am talking about – He is there! God is in a special place – in the midst of my busyness. He's in the blessing zone.

Just as God is there in the midst of our busyness, He is there when we ask Him to reveal His plan for us and He seems to be silent. When you feel like you are in a holding pattern or that you've been put on a shelf, He is there. Continue to walk by faith. Wherever you go and whatever you do, allow God's love to flow through you. Proverbs 3:5-6 NKJV tells us, *Trust in the Lord with all your heart, and lean not to your own understanding; In all your ways acknowledge Him, and He shall direct your paths.* Acknowledge His presence in your daily life – for wherever you are, He is. God is in a special place – in the midst of my busyness and in His silence. This is the special place where I know, unequivocally, that He is there. In the blessing zone, from wall to wall, ceiling to floor, God is there. He fills the room with the richness of who He is. After all, He is God Almighty. *Now to Him Who is able to do immeasurably more than all we ask or imagine, according to His power that is at work within us* (Ephesians 3:20 NIV).

How do you find your Blessing Zone?

Philippians 4:8 NIV says, *Finally, brothers and sisters, whatever is true, whatever is noble, whatever is right, whatever is pure, whatever is lovely, whatever is admirable – if anything is excellent or praiseworthy – think about such things.* When you meditate on those things which are good, you find the peace of God. Instead of focusing on being busy, we need to reflect on those good things that bring us joy –

those noble things, those lovely things, and those things that are of good report. I have reminders of those "things" in the photo album on my iPad. I have a collection of photos stored, and I have learned to use them to help me remember those lovely things in life that bring me joy. Spending time with my grandson brings me immense joy. My grandson strolling through the Phoenix Zoo having a chat with Mr. Monkey and Dr. Giraffe – what a joy! Papa and our grandson musing about who is going to have the last word on the topic of the day – what a joy! Remembering those moments immediately takes me to the blessing zone.

My photos from the Victorious Women's Conference bring me great joy! Women, hungering for the Word of God, were blessed through the teachings during the conference – what joy! We were in a workshop titled, *Facing Your Giants: Dealing with Anger*. There we sat in a room, a group of women with underlying issues related to anger: broken relationships, disappointment, wayward children, inconsiderate husbands, dashed hopes, unfulfilled dreams and, yes, careers derailed by an unstable economic environment. The photos tell the story – before and after. I see transformation in those photos. I see growth in those photos. I see wisdom in those photos. I see women who found their blessing zone – at last! What joy! I see my own transformation! I didn't think I had anger issues. God wrapped this workshop into a package that persuaded me to attend so that I could watch others get blessed. But I soon found out that I needed that workshop as much, if not more, than everyone else in attendance. Participants were blessed and, indeed, so was I. We found our blessing zone! The photos were a reminder of the Great Transformer who allowed our transformation. *And do not be conformed to this world, but be transformed by the renewing of your mind, that you may prove what is that good and acceptable and perfect will of God.* (Romans 12:2 NKJV)

Finally, every morning in my solitude, I spend time with the Lord through the reading of His life's story – His love letter to me – the Bible. I love this time. It brings me great joy. Waking up to a new day, which is a gift from God, brings me joy! Reading a chapter of Proverbs each morning brings me joy. Committing another day to God's plan is a place of joy! Regardless of what the day may bring forth, I know that the Lord is there and I am in the blessing zone.

You can find your own blessing zone. You need not look far – it is right there in front of you. Lay aside your busyness, your juggles, and your struggles. Feel the presence of the Lord. It may be the nudge you sense as you are comforting a loved one. It may be the breeze you feel as you think about an important job decision. It may be the tug you experience when asked to join a ministry or Bible study. It could be a tap on the shoulder to accept a responsibility that you have no idea about how you could ever do it. The tap is the catalyst to say yes – to get beyond your comfort zone – to move into your blessing zone. Be bold, make a move, honor God, and allow His blessings to overflow in your life! Discover your blessing zone, which is custom designed just for you!

The Blessing Zone in a Time of Challenge

We live in a fallen world. God has not promised that we will not have trials and tribulations. Indeed, we will. As we live and serve the Lord, life happens and it doesn't always go as planned. A dear friend of mine has a plaque on her wall that reads "We plan, God laughs." This is so true. Our best laid out plans can be shifted in the twinkling of an eye. Job losses, a prodigal child, an aging parent, unpaid bills, a bad report from the doctor, or an automobile accident are all examples of unplanned events that can change our lives suddenly. The example provided by Paul is an illustration of a period of trials and tribulations:

2 Corinthians 1:8-9 NKJV says, *For we do not want you to be ignorant, brethren, of our trouble which came to us in Asia: that we were burdened beyond measure, above strength, so that we despaired even of life. Yes, we had the sentence of death in ourselves, that we should not trust in ourselves but in God Who raises the dead.*

There is good news -- Jesus rules and He is on the throne! During our most challenging trials, Jesus is there! In our most difficult tribulations, Jesus is there! He is our protector, our fortress, and our refuge!

Psalm 91:1-6 NKJV says, *He who dwells in the secret place of the Most High shall abide under the shadow of the Almighty. I will say of the Lord, "He is my refuge and my fortress; my God, in Him I will trust." Surely He shall deliver you from the snare of the fowler, and from the perilous pestilence. He shall cover you with His feathers, and under His wings you shall take refuge; His truth shall be your shield and buckler. You shall not be afraid of the terror by night, nor of the arrow that flies by day, nor of the pestilence that walks in darkness, nor of the destruction that lays waste at noonday.*

In the midst of our trials, God is there. The tribulations draw us closer to Him. We put our trust in Him. God is the master planner and the master of all. The key is to know Him intimately so that when the trial comes, and it will, you have an established relationship with the Lord and He will carry you through. When you have a report that shakes you to your core, you are prepared because He is with you. God knew about the report before you ever received it. He saw you as He hung on the cross. He laid down His life so that we may have life more abundantly. As we travel through life's trials and tribulations, we can and will get to our blessing zone. Indeed, we can experience our own blessing zone, even in the midst of the trial. This is possible because the Lord is with us – and, as such, wherever God is, is the same place of our blessing zone!

Pearls of Wisdom

Consider the following pearls of wisdom as you begin your discovery journey to the blessing zone:

- **Enrich your life.** Acknowledge that the blessing zone is a real place.
- **Explore God's plan.** Appreciate the Master's plan.
- **Engage with God.** Align yourself with His love letter to you – the Bible.
- **Experience the richness of the blessing zone.** Attend to God's presence. He is always there.
- **Enhance your relationship with Him.** Accept His goodness and, in times of trial and tribulation, you will be glad you did.

- **Expand your vision to see your blessing zone.** Apply what is needed from your journey to create your divinely inspired vision of your blessing zone.

After Glow

The blessing zone is a real place – a source of joy, peace, comfort, and love. Busyness can camouflage our blessing zone. The juggles and struggles of life can make it seem like the blessing zone does not exist. There are many life experiences that provide snippets of our blessing zone. It's important that we open our hearts to the nudges, pushes, catalysts, challenges, trials, and tribulations that create the tapestry of understanding that comes our way.

James 1:2-4 NKJV says, *My brethren, count it all joy when you fall into various trials, knowing that the testing of your faith produces patience. But let patience have its perfect work, that you may be perfect and complete, lacking nothing.*

When we open our hearts to see the vision of the blessing zone, it comes into full view. We learn through the pearls of wisdom that the Lord will meet us where we are and create in us a passion to discover our unique blessing zone. During those times of joy and times of challenge, there are many opportunities to discover hints of God's purpose and plan for us. Now is the time to open your heart. God will take you where you need to be to discover your blessing zone.

Chapter 1: Discover Your Blessing Zone!
Notes

THE BLESSING ZONE

Chapter 2: Enrich Your Life

Acknowledge The Blessing Zone As a Real Place

My spiritual journey began when I was around 11 years old. Late one Friday evening, I was home alone. My mother and stepfather had decided to visit family and friends that evening. My youngest sister went with them. My older brother and sister decided to visit their friends, leaving me home alone, looking for something to do. I was always afraid of being alone. My extroversion created the opportunity to engage with others as much as possible. I recognized the need to be with others very early in life.

While home alone that evening, the blessing zone did not appear to be within reach. In fact, it was a very distant place; however, I felt the need that evening to draw closer to that special place. I did not have a relationship with the Lord. I knew that He was real and that in His presence, I was in a blessed place – the blessing zone.

My mother talked about God often. She listened to her "spirituals" on Sunday evenings as she ironed for the week. I remember nesting myself under the ironing board to be close to my mother, listening to her "spirituals" as well. I remembered songs like "Blessed Assurance" and "What a Friend We Have in Jesus." Certainly, there was not much context for these songs since we rarely attended church; but I knew there was something special about Jesus. To an unchurched 11 year old, I was curious but didn't know why. There was profound recognition that my special seat under the ironing board was indeed a place of peace, comfort, and joy.

So there alone on a Friday evening, it was important that I find something to do. I needed to find a way to entertain myself and get over my anxiety of being alone. I needed to enrich my life. We lived in a rough neighborhood at the time and home burglaries were frequent. My strategy was to leave the front and back doors of the house open. I believed that by leaving both doors open, if a burglar came into the front door, I could run out of the back door to safety. The same thinking also supported a back door intrusion. In looking back, it is clear that this was not an effective strategy! Thankfully, God had another plan that evening. It was a plan to draw me closer to Him.

Jeremiah 29:11 NIV says, *"For I know the plans I have for you," declares the LORD, "plans to prosper you and not to harm you, plans to give you a hope and a future."*

There was an old, portable record player in the closet located near the front door. The record player was very popular for music in the 1960s. This particular record player was left in the trash of a neighbor and quickly became a treasure to our family. As it turned out that evening, there were several records from the Top Ten list. There was one record of faith. This was the record that drew my attention.

I retrieved the record player from the closet. There was an electrical outlet near the front door, which aligned with my strategy – intruders in the front door, run to safety out the back door. The record was titled "Lord You Brought Me from a Mighty Long Way" by the Five Blind Boys. I had heard this song previously from my nest under my mother's ironing board. I plugged in the power cord, dusted off the record, placed the record on the turntable, and turned on the power. Little did I know that I had truly plugged into the power of God. I had discovered that the blessing zone is a real place – it is when we are in the presence of the Lord and aligned with His plan and purpose.

The record player was not an automatic record player, where the arm of the player would automatically and precisely land at the very beginning of the record. This record player required a manual function. I had to place the arm of the record player on the record with precision to ensure that the music started correctly. I was hooked at the first verse.

The strength of the lyrics stirred me so that I was compelled to listen to the song over and over again. Each time the record played, I listened for greater understanding. The warmth of the Lord was right there with me. I was in a real place of blessing. The Lord was there and I felt such peace – it was overwhelming. Tears flowed and there was no explanation why – but God. I believed that the Lord sent His protection to me that evening. For the first time, I wanted to know this God. The Holy Spirit stirred me that evening. I wanted to know this God of the song. I wanted to stay in His presence. I wanted to be in the center of His blessing zone.

Psalm 37:4 NKJV says, *Delight yourself also in the LORD, And He shall give you the desires of your heart.*

Hours passed quickly as the song played again and again. Time passed so quickly that when my family returned home close to midnight, the song was still playing. The muscles in my frail hand were painful from all the manual movement to get the arm of the record player in the precise location to ensure I could hear the song from beginning to end. That evening, it was clear that I had discovered that the blessing zone is a real place. It was an important step for me. I drew nearer to God and He drew nearer to me.

Chapter 2: Enrich Your Life
Notes

THE BLESSING ZONE

Chapter 3: Explore God's Plan
Appreciate the Master's Plan

There is a master plan for us all. Sometimes, life's circumstances stimulate us to put our own plan of action in place rather than talking with God about His plan. It takes endurance to remain steadfast, trusting the Lord's plan – even when our preference is to do things our way. God's plan is better. God has created His plan for our path, our journey, our road to glorify Him. There will be trials and tribulations; but we must know that, through it all, we have victory in Jesus.

Maria's story of the Master's plan is an important life lesson to me.

Thalidomide was a drug used in the late 1950s and early 1960s to relieve the effects of morning sickness in pregnant women. The drug was widely used in Australia, Europe, and Japan with limited use in the United States. The drug never received approval for use by the Federal Drug Administration; however, several expectant mothers did use the drug since it was available for testing purposes. One side effect of the drug was limb reduction anomalies, as well congenital heart disease. Maria was born with these anomalies. Maria shared her story of the Master's plan that provided the opportunity to capture the grace and mercy of God. The foundation of her story is a reminder to appreciate the Master's plan – even in the midst of great challenges.

Maria's mobility was amazing. She could come and go on a scooter that was designed for people with anomalies created by the Thalidomide drug. Her physical challenges never served as a barrier to the plans God had for her life.

Maria successfully secured employment with General Motors Corporation and worked there for more than 25 years. This was when I first met her – and this is another validation of an appreciation for God's plan through the relationship of others. Maria had many health challenges, yet she chose to focus on her possibilities rather than what may have appeared to be impossible for others. Maria's personality was bright, cheery, and positive. She became an expert in technology and handled her reporting responsibility with care. Maria wanted to be involved in all activities at work and made a point to be included in planning to ensure all technology factors were considered.

I recall visiting Maria in the hospital during one of her many stays due to her health challenges. As we visited, Maria talked about all the plans she had to contribute to the success of the department. She wanted to use technology more to improve the efficiency and effectiveness of processes and systems within the Human Resources organization. Maria fiddled with the oxygen mask because it was getting in her way of talking about the future. I looked at Maria and was amazed at her appreciation for life, her perseverance, and her endurance. Maria was not going to let this hospital visit get in the way of her appreciation for God's plans for her life.

Maria enjoyed discussing her vision and how she could have a positive impact for a more efficient department. She didn't know why she was faced with her current physical challenges; however, she knew that she was in the divine plan of God. I prayed with Maria that evening during the visit and realized that the tests Maria faced through her health challenges became her testimony. A testimony centered in her endurance for the race the Lord had crafted just for her.

Maria had many friends and a very supportive family. In addition, she married Donald and enjoyed being a wife and friend to him. Maria had an uncanny desire to help others in need. She frequently stopped by my office to ask if there was anything I needed, since she was in the neighborhood often. Keep in mind, Maria was required to securely fasten herself to her mobile scooter – which was no small task – to gain mobility to move from one location to another. Her delightful and extraverted personality provided the motivation to endure through her physical challenges, touching the hearts of others by her need to help.

My relationship with Maria grew over time. The appreciation for God's plan for Maria's life unfolded gently in the midst of our time together. Maria allowed me to pray with her and, during these times of prayer, we entered the blessing zone, right in the middle of God's plan. God loved Maria and Maria loved Him. As we pondered God's love, I was reminded that He was in the midst of our encounters. I knew that God would always be there for Maria.

Romans 8:35-39 NKJV says, *Who shall separate us from the love of Christ? Shall tribulation, or distress, or persecution, or famine, or nakedness, or peril, or sword? As it is written: "For Your sake we are killed all day long; we are accounted as sheep for the slaughter." Yet in all these things we are more than conquerors through Him Who loved us. For I am persuaded that neither death nor life, nor angels nor principalities nor powers, nor things present nor things to come, nor height nor depth, nor any other created thing, shall be able to separate us from the love of God which is in Christ Jesus our Lord.*

Maria's health challenges were chronic. During her final days on this earth, she was repeatedly hospitalized for chronic respiratory ailments. Maria attended a Christmas party I hosted for the department. I remember calling ahead to the restaurant so that arrangements could be made for Maria to be seated comfortably at the table. It was a grand event. Maria appeared with a smile that truly touched my heart. She had a Christmas gift for me and it hung on the handle of her scooter, swinging to and fro as she drove her scooter to the table. I remember thinking about the challenge of Christmas shopping for Maria, and yet she wanted to be a blessing to me. At that moment, I saw an appreciation for God's plan by the honor of a friendship with Maria.

Maria's story of endurance is certainly a demonstration of overcoming the challenges of life. Through her trials and tribulations, I look back and can see God's master plan for her life. I see the many contributions that Maria made in the lives of others – contributions of service, contributions of courage, and contributions of giving.

I learned the following lessons from Maria's life:

- Live every day with courage, joy, and peace.
- See obstacles as opportunities to show God's mercy and grace.
- Give to others and see giving as an opening to plant seeds of hope.
- Recognize the power of relationships, with God and with others.
- Embrace the love that only comes from God.
- Stay the course. Keep it moving!
- Appreciate the Master's plan and endure the race set before you.

Hebrews 12:1-2 NKJV says, *Therefore we also, since we are surrounded by so great a cloud of witnesses, let us lay aside every weight, and the sin which so easily ensnares us, and let us run with endurance the race that is set before us, looking unto Jesus, the author and finisher of our faith, Who for the joy that was set before Him endured the cross, despising the shame, and has sat down at the right hand of the throne of God.*

In the blessing zone, we appreciate the Master's plan.

Chapter 3: Explore God's Plan
Notes

THE BLESSING ZONE

Chapter 4: Engage with God

The move to Phoenix was challenging indeed. This was a new opportunity with many new discoveries on the horizon. The move was triggered by a job offer that sounded intriguing. There were only two complications. The first complication was that my husband was not enamored with Phoenix. David enjoyed the four seasons and was not enthused about two seasons: warm weather for five months and hot weather for the remainder of the year. David provided the support needed through the decision-making process, and we collectively made the decision that I should take the job in Phoenix. During my doctoral studies, there were five residency requirements, and the location was in Phoenix. As a result of the residency requirements, Phoenix became familiar and I created a network with other students.

The second complication was that the person who hired me decided to leave the organization prior to my start date. This was clearly a dilemma. There were significant accountabilities with the assignment, as well as the need to drive change in the organization. Strategically, gaining insights on the cultural nuances as well as key stakeholders was essential to effectively integrate into the organization. Without the hiring manager's support, the loneliness factor emerged.

In light of life's complications, a renewed interest in drawing closer to God unfolded. I conversed with the Lord in my vehicle as I traveled to and from the office. I hosted praise and worship services in my home – with just me and the Lord. The more I engaged with God, the more He engaged with me. His presence was with me all the time. I had an irresistible need to raise my hands in praise. I could feel the sweetness of His presence. I was again in the blessing zone. Through the trials of loneliness and finding my way around in a new city, starting a new job in a new industry, and developing new networks, God was there all along. My vehicle became a blessing zone. My home became a blessing zone. I engaged with God, and He engaged with me.

Psalm 34:4 NKJV says, *I sought the LORD, and He heard me, and delivered me from all my fears.*

I visited several churches in my first year in Phoenix. It was certainly good to be assembled with other believers. One of the most important lessons I learned was the need to continue to move forward with this chapter of my life. Having never lived alone, I discovered how much I enjoyed the companionship of marriage.

David and I made it a point to talk every day, and we seemed to have much more to discuss than when we were actually in the same location. He caught me up on what was going on with family in Michigan and the weather reports, which were vastly different between Michigan and Arizona, new happenings at our church home in Michigan, as well as updates from our neighborhood. I talked about my search for a new church home in Arizona, new friendships, new organizations, as well as updates on the new job.

Technology played an interesting role as well. I learned to Skype as well as how to use FaceTime on my iPad. This helped me stay connected to my family, and, in particular, my grandson. It was always good to hear him say, "Hi Grammy!" We had conversations about his day, his friends, and sometimes even took time for a bedtime story. My daughter also provided updates about her life and plans for the week. Our conversations generally occurred on a Sunday afternoon. Our conversations seemed much more meaningful, and I always felt a sense of completeness following our discussions. Loneliness seemed to subside as a result of those Sunday afternoon conversations.

The truth is that the relocation to Phoenix created additional time to engage with God. It also created additional time for engagement with family. What became clear is that engagement is a choice.

James 4:8 NKJV tells us, *Draw near to God and He will draw near to you.*

Lessons learned from engaging with God:

- God is always there, waiting for us to draw nearer.
- Times of loneliness create superb opportunities to engage with God if we open our hearts to Him.

- Seize opportunities to engage with God – not just when all is well. Sometimes, the best opportunities emerge during times of trial.
- Seek clarity of God's plans, purpose, and passion that He designed specifically for you.
- Trust God always as His path for you unfolds.

The transition to Phoenix presented an amazing path – one that was truly designed by God. New friendships, new relationships, and more opportunities continued to develop. Engagement with God during my time of transition and loneliness laid the foundation for the blessing zone in yet a new and profound way.

Chapter 4: Engage with God
Notes

THE BLESSING ZONE

Chapter 5: Experience the Richness of the Blessing Zone

Trust the Lord to abundantly bless, for great is His faithfulness! God's calling for us is to experience His richness in the blessing zone through stewardship, significance, and success! God is not just present in our lives; He is active and powerful. He is doing a mighty work in light of His unconditional love for us.

Many have been a blessing to the ministry of Victorious Women. The ministry works with organizations who serve families who are generally underserved. The prayer is that the Lord returns to donors a hundredfold for the seeds sown in the ministry of Victorious Women. Through the richness of His blessings, hundreds of families have had their needs met through the organization. It is amazing how the Lord continues to expand our ability to increase the numbers of families served, even during economic challenges throughout the country. I know that only God can do that and, through the willingness of supporters of Victorious Women, He accomplishes great things. It has been a collective effort, trusting the Lord to put His supernatural with our natural resources to experience the richness of the blessing zone. Our Lord is stunning!

The Lord shows up. I take no credit for this. It is the Lord Who shows up in the hearts of contributors and serves as a catalyst to move them into action. This action stimulates movement into the blessing zone – to be a blessing to others. Contributors make the decision to be a blessing to a child or adult at his or her time of need. It is so profound how the Lord works so perfectly in ensuring that the needs of others are met. He only gives us stewardship over this effort. He trusts us enough to manage this ministry for His glory and to experience the richness of the blessing zone.

I recently met with an organization to discuss some ideas regarding expansion of the ministry. During the meeting, the spokesperson shared the significance of Victorious Women. It was revealed to me by the Holy Spirit that this *is* a ministry of significance. It's not about letting the ministry shine but letting Him shine through the ministry. There is a tendency to look at the small number of people being served; however, through the eyes of those we are blessing, it a blessing of great significance. It is an opportunity to experience the richness of the blessing zone. In most cases, the blessings of the donations offered by this ministry represent the sum of what the families receive during the Christmas holiday season. Christmas is about Jesus; not about the gifts. We are clear about that. But the families who are recipients of our gifts and donations see the light of Jesus through our caring actions.

I recently had the opportunity to hear a message at church regarding how others will see Jesus in our lives. As we listened to the message, Pastor Mike shared that others will see Jesus through our love. We learned that for those who are unchurched or have not come to know the reality of Jesus as Lord and Savior, we can be a vessel of God's love. Our acts of kindness are expressions of the love that only comes from Jesus. Our willingness to bless someone that we do not know, in light of the challenges we may be facing, is another amazing action of God. This amazing action takes us to the blessing zone to experience His richness.

I am acting on what the Lord has placed on my heart regarding His expectations for me. I am here to serve Him in the capacity of ministries to women and families. By way of background, Victorious Women was born in 2011 out of another ministry, Women in Christ. Women in Christ was founded in 1998 as a result of a small group of women coming together to grow in their relationship with the Lord. We searched the Scriptures, seeking answers to circumstances in which we were challenged. It started with attending a women's Christian conference, United Conference for Women. Several of us gathered after Day 1 of the conference in a hotel room. We started to discuss an issue and someone piped in and said, "Let's see what the Word has to say about that." At that moment, Women in Christ was born. We were up in the wee hours of the night searching, discussing, and learning about what the Lord had to say about our challenges – and believe me, He had a lot to say! The next phase of the ministry expanded into a book club, where we read books written by Christian authors and discussed revelations that were disclosed to us through the book. We also invited friends to join us in our book club. We expanded beyond just reading the selected book but also searching the Scriptures to determine God's view as well. We continued to grow in our relationship with the Lord and deepened our walk with Him through understanding revealed in His Word. Truly, we experienced the richness of God in the blessing zone.

Our focus on meeting the needs of families in crisis has always been a priority for Victorious Women. I was drawn to such organizations and have come to know why. It is the work of such organizations that specifically serve women and families that tugs at my heart strings. I am reminded that the Lord uniquely and specifically created those heart strings for me. The results of this ministry have been directly related to the grace of God. Year after year, over the course of several years, the number of families blessed by Women in Christ, which later became Victorious Women, has increased. At the birth of the ministry, the economy was flourishing. As we know, the economy can flounder and yet the ministry continues to develop and expand. In the business world, this equals success. In God's world, I believe He sets the foundation for our growth – praise God! This is another amazing action of the Lord!

A new beginning for Victorious Women was initiated in 2012 with our first Victorious Women's Conference Cruise. It served as a profound opportunity to experience the richness of the blessing zone.

To prepare thoroughly for this experience, participants were asked to lay aside 10 minutes every day leading up to the conference cruise to pray for the following:

- God's plan to unfold in a way that brings Him honor and that His will be done.
- To pray for each speaker – that the Lord provides His wisdom, strength, courage, and power to unleash everything He has

for us during this experience as provided through the chosen vessels.

- To pray for the administrative team – that all planning goes extremely well.
- To pray for an experience without barriers. We want smooth seas, calm winds, great weather, and God's peace.
- We pray for a delightful experience as we travel to Miami, to all cruise destinations, and as we return safely to our homes.
- To pray for excellent health and direction for all who are on the cruise, including the captain and his team, as well as the other cruisers.

Victorious Women hosted its first Conference Cruise aboard Royal Caribbean's Majesty of the Seas. The event included 108 women from across the country, who enjoyed three days of spiritual activities. Hebrews 12:1-2 NKJV was chosen as the over-arching Scripture, supporting the theme: *Let us run with endurance the race that is set before us, looking unto Jesus, the author and finisher of our faith.* The dynamic team included Elder Sheila Vann (Second Ebenezer Church, Detroit, Michigan), Priscilla Archangel, Ph.D. (Faith Centered Leadership, Plymouth, Michigan), Sharon Allison-Ottey, MD (Health Strategist, Physician, Educator and Author, Baltimore, Maryland), Evangelist Janice Hill (A Harvest of Souls Ministries, Livonia Michigan), and Victoria Jones, DM, (Victorious Women Ministries, Michigan and Arizona). Each speaker inspired participants with a powerful message of spiritually enlightened wisdom regarding God's uniquely appointed race.

Elder Vann opened the conference with a commanding message regarding staying focused on God's plan and the importance of becoming a K.I.M. (Keep it Moving) sister. Dr. Sharon's workshop centered on wellness and the impact of health during the race of endurance. Dr. Archangel's workshop underscored biblical examples of the key to staying grounded in God's Word during the race of endurance. Evangelist Hill's message provided deep insights on staying the course during the endurance race as established by the Lord. Finally, Dr. Jones provided an endurance framework that can be used as a resource beyond the conference. Conference attendees enjoyed a victory run each morning to set the course of the day. The conference team clearly added richness to the blessing zone.

The culminating event was an impactful altar call led by Elder Vann, who offered prayer and anointing. It was a spiritually charged experience that had a transformational impact on participants. One such participant commented that, "This is the most spiritually rich event I have ever attended."

I conclude this message with Scripture:

> *Blessed be the God and Father of our Lord Jesus Christ, Who has blessed us with every spiritual blessing in the heavenly places in Christ.* (Ephesians 1:3 NKJV)

May you experience the richness of the blessing zone today!

Chapter 5: Experience the Richness of The Blessing Zone
Notes

THE BLESSING ZONE

Chapter 6: Enhance Your Relationship with Him

This story began in January of 2008 when I was on a business trip to China – a trip that lasted two months. In planning for the trip, I was busy determining what clothing to take, staying in the same color family to maximize my ability to mix and match, deciding on what shoes to take since I would be teaching extensively, and deciding which Bible to take with me for my journey. I decided to take my NIV Bible rather than my Study Bible, which is NKJV. That was a wise decision. It was going to be a long trip, requiring me to be diligent about my job assignment of teaching leadership principles to leaders in China.

I also had to prepare for the many cultural differences between the U.S. and China, all the while praying for God's strength to exercise great wisdom in my engagement with the Chinese. As I packed, I found a special place in my luggage for my Bible. I pondered how I would do without the ability to fellowship with other Christians while in China. This was a factor that I completely underestimated. It was a challenge that engulfed me with uncertainty. I continued to press forward with my packing.

As I packed, I started to think about being without my family for such a long time. I thought to myself, *How will my husband fend for himself? How will my daughter and son-in-law do without me?* My mother was showing early signs of dementia, and I wondered what she would remember, if anything, upon my return. As I continued to pack, the tears started to flow and I knew, at that moment, this situation was completely in the Lord's hands. I did not have the answers; however, I knew Who did! I knew that the Lord had a love for me like no other – a love that was so deep and that was, and continues to be, unconditional. I could not see the path in front of me. I knew I had to take this step of faith. I so desperately needed to feel the love of the Lord in this adventure that was before me and His reassurance that all was well; however, that love and reassurance felt beyond my reach. I knew from the Word of God that He loved me. I just needed to have that truth deepened in my spirit. That deepening was yet to come -- to enhance my relationship with Him.

While in China, I was quite busy meeting business leaders, government officials, and my General Motors' colleagues who were there to support the project related to leadership development. The weekdays were filled with meetings, training events, and dinner plans. The days were long, 12-15 hours per day. Weekends included exploring the country of China and its fascinating history and culture. On Sundays, I longed for fellowship in a local church; however, it was not to be – at least not until toward the end of my trip. Buddhism is the primary religion of China. China was, and continues to be, a mission field for Christianity. As weeks passed by, my longing continued to grow. It was an amazing experience to go to bookstores, shops, open markets, neighborhoods, and communities and not see signs of Christianity. My Bible became such a comfort to me, yet I longed for more. I grew into a state of anxiety, which concerned me tremendously. I asked the Lord for help, and it came in an interesting and powerful way.

A local colleague from work, who I will call Esther, sent me an email and asked if I would have lunch with her on Saturday. I had been in China for close to two months and found weekends very difficult. I happily accepted Esther's invitation for the coming Saturday.

Esther arrived early Saturday morning, and we took a taxi to one of her favorite shopping locations. We shopped and we enjoyed an authentic Chinese lunch that afternoon. Esther and I later returned to my hotel, and I invited her to have tea with me prior to her departure.

As we enjoyed our tea and cookies, Esther shared with me that she was having trouble with her supervisor and was quite upset with his behavior. I asked Esther to share more. As Esther's story unfolded, it was a clear case of sexual harassment. Esther shared that her supervisor indicated that if she cooperated with him, he would not be so demanding. Esther shared with me that she was a "good" Chinese girl and did not want to give in to the requests of her supervisor. She wept, and I felt her distress.

Esther then shared that she had tried everything to handle the situation. She had repeatedly prayed to Buddha, but her prayers had not been answered. The door of love opened to me at that very moment, and I remembered John 3:16 NKJV: *For God so loved the world that He gave His only begotten Son, that whoever believes in Him should not perish but have life everlasting.* Those words swept over me like a mighty river, and suddenly the anxiety I was feeling during those months in China started to lift.

I shared with Esther that I knew the Savior of the world. Esther asked, Who is He? I told Esther that His name is Jesus. I witnessed to Esther about the love of the Lord and my relationship with Him. I shared how God sent Jesus to save us, because all of us are sinners. I also shared that Jesus went to a place called Calvary and was crucified for our sins. I shared that the story did not end there. I shared that Jesus died on the cross for us that we might be reconciled to God. Our reconciliation to God allows us life everlasting for those who accept Jesus as Lord and Savior. I also shared that Jesus rose from the dead after three days, defeating death. Esther pondered our discussion and was quite intrigued. We ended our conversation with a word of prayer, and I was suddenly grateful to God for all that I had experienced in China, up until my Saturday with Esther. I shared information with Esther regarding my church in Michigan and how I missed the fellowship with others who believed.

Esther departed from our conversation with a hug and thanked me for making her aware of Jesus. This was the beginning of the blessing zone. It was also a glorious opportunity to expand my relationship with the Lord.

I was so starved for the fellowship of other believers, I decided to reach out to a Christian colleague and friend in the U.S. who had visited China in the past. I asked my friend Priscilla if she was aware of a Christian church in Shanghai, China. Priscilla indicated that she knew of a church called Abundant Grace International Fellowship. Even though Priscilla had not visited the church personally, she had heard good things about it, and she knew it was a teaching ministry based upon the Word of God. My heart grew with excitement and I felt the presence of the Holy Spirit. The blessing zone continued to unfold.

Immediately, I sent an email to Esther letting her know about Abundant Grace. Esther was so happy and wanted to attend the church with me. She wanted to know more about Jesus. Of course, the tears came and I suddenly realized that I was on mission – not a mission just to teach leadership principles to young Chinese leaders but on a mission to introduce a young woman by the name of Esther to the love of the Lord. That was the path I could not see as I was packing for the trip, preparing for a journey of uncertainty. God continuously whispered to me, *"Victoria...I have a plan and I love you."* God knew the path and the plan. His Word says so in Jeremiah 29:11 NIV: *"For I know the plans I have for you," declares the LORD, "plans to prosper you and not to harm you, plans to give you hope and a future."*

So Esther and I prepared to attend Sunday service at Abundant Grace. I planned for Esther to meet me at the hotel and we would take a taxi from there. Little did I know that Esther had another plan. She arrived at the hotel at 9 a.m. to allow for travel to Abundant Grace. Service started at 10 a.m. Upon Esther's arrival, I discovered that she was driving a car which she shared with her brother. In China, a car was quite a luxury as bicycles represented the major mode of transportation. I learned during our trip to Abundant Grace that this was Esther's maiden voyage. The car had been purchased a week ago, and this was Esther's first time driving. My heart skipped a beat.

I had provided Esther with the address of Abundant Grace, and she mapped out the trip prior to her arrival at the hotel. The only problem was that, somehow, Esther's mapping was not quite accurate. My zeal for attending Abundant Grace and to introduce Esther to further exposure to Jesus seemed to calm my fears in this driving experience. As we traveled, suddenly, I realized that Esther was lost and I began to pray. As I was praying, Esther turned down a one-way street going in the wrong direction – God certainly has a sense of humor! As God instructed me not to make Esther nervous, I calmly advised Esther that she was traveling down a one-way street in the wrong direction. She immediately turned around to travel in the right direction. There was yet another challenge forthcoming. Somehow, Esther ended up driving on railroad tracks, and with some coaching we were back on the road. Then suddenly, Esther turned the corner and there it was – a single-story brick building with a cross on the front of the building. I knew that had to be Abundant Grace and my eyes filled with tears. I knew that the Lord had shown us abundant grace in our travels to get to the church. When I saw the cross, the Holy Spirit swept over me. I felt the presence of the Lord and His great love for me, and His great love for Esther. We parked and entered the church. We were greeted with a love so sweet, it took my breath away. I was entering into the blessing zone.

I was reminded of words from Pastor Mike during a sermon he taught when I first arrived at North Ridge, my new church since relocating to Phoenix in January of 2009. Pastor Mike ministered on love and asked the question, "How will people know that you are a believer?" He answered his question to the congregation with this: "They will know it by the love that you show." The love of those who greeted Esther and me was overwhelming. I was so happy that Esther could experience this real love for herself. This is a love that comes from Jesus Christ alone. As we took our seats, a four-member praise team walked to the front of the stage and began singing a very familiar song, Give Thanks with a Grateful Heart.

As the lyrics filled the air, tears of joy flowed down my face – oh, how sweet was the blessing zone. I looked at Esther and tears flowed down her cheeks as well. In the stillness of that moment, Esther and I embraced, and I personally knew the love of the Lord in a much deeper way than ever before. It was as though Jesus whispered in my ear, *"P.S. I love you."* Esther and I were in the blessing zone.

Then the Word of God was ministered by Pastor Nate Showalter, who served as senior pastor of Abundant Grace. The message of the morning was titled "Master Evangelist." As I listened and was inspired by the ministry coming from Pastor Nate, I marveled at how the Lord had so perfectly arranged all of the events of my two-month stay in China. Pastor Nate talked about our responsibility of evangelism as instructed by Jesus in His great commission to us in Matthew 28:19-20 NKJV: *"Go therefore and make disciples of all the nations, baptizing them in the name of the Father, and of the Son and of the Holy Spirit, teaching them to observe all things that I have commanded you; and lo, I am with you always, even to the end of the age."* As I read Scripture along with Pastor Nate in my Bible, Esther leaned close so that she could read along, too. I was grateful to the Lord that I had brought my NIV Bible as the translation is a bit easier to understand for the novice. The tears came again and I felt God's embrace and His whisper. The Lord had covered every detail. Only God could know that a conversation over tea and cookies between two friends and work colleagues could turn into a story so powerful that it would put us in the midst of the blessing zone.

As we left the service, Esther and I enjoyed a powerful fellowship with members of Abundant Grace. I shared my love for women's ministries when I was asked about my interests in the church. I was introduced to the director of the women's ministries, Victoria Piekenpol. Victoria was quite lovely. She shared the current events happening with the women's ministry. It was a delightful fellowship, and I introduced Esther to Victoria in hopes of an emerging relationship. This exchange also enhanced my relationship with God as I saw the glory of His plan unfold.

As Esther and I departed, we waved goodbye to the fine members of Abundant Grace. We thoroughly enjoyed our time there, and Victoria promised to connect with Esther going forward. Esther, of course, had many questions during our drive back to the hotel – which by the way was incident-free. Esther dropped me off at the hotel and continued on her way to afternoon activities with her family. The following week, I departed from Shanghai, China, to return to the States. On my last day in China, Esther came to the hotel to say farewell. As we hugged and said our goodbyes, Esther whispered in my ear, "I am finding my way to Jesus."

That was the last time I saw Esther. Subsequently, I have received a Christmas card from Esther every year. The card always read: *Victoria, Merry Christmas and God's best in the coming New Year. Love, your daughter, Esther.* I am not sure if Esther continued to connect with Abundant Grace. I do know that the Lord loves Esther and that He used me as His vessel to introduce her to Christ. Together, we entered the blessing zone on that very special Sunday. I kept the church program from Abundant Grace. On the front of the program, it reads: "Far more than we dare ask or imagine." My experience there was just that! The Lord truly exceeded my expectations.

This experience represented God's gift to me. I am reminded of two Scriptures:

John 3:16 NKJV: *For God so loved the world that He gave His only begotten Son, that whoever believes in Him should not perish but have everlasting life.*

Romans 8:37-39 NKJV: *Yet in all these things we are more than conquerors through Him Who loved us. For I am persuaded that neither death nor life, nor angels nor principalities nor powers, nor things present nor things to come, nor height nor depth, nor any other created thing, shall be able to separate us from the love of God which is in Christ Jesus our Lord.*

A month later after returning to the States, Esther emailed me with good news. Esther was recruited away to another company with enhanced pay and benefits shortly after our prayer time in China. Esther very much enjoys her new employer – another demonstration that God does indeed answer prayer.

While in China, I was lonely and longing for a deeper relationship with the Lord. God fulfilled His plan for His mission in a deep and profound way. As I traveled home, the Lord whispered in my ear, "P.S. I love you!" I am grateful for that! It was truly a grand blessing zone experience. Indeed, my relationship with the Lord was enhanced in a powerful and mighty way.

Chapter 6: Enhance Your Relationship with Him

Notes

THE BLESSING ZONE

Chapter 7: Expand Your Vision to See Your Blessing Zone

Change is hard. We like being in our respective comfort zones. To see the fullness of God, it is necessary to expand our vision. This requires change, and change is hard.

For 36 years, General Motors was my employer, and I truly enjoyed the many marvelous opportunities afforded to me. I elected to retire from the company in November of 2008.

It was a privilege to work for General Motors as a Human Resources leader and professional. The challenging decision to retire was fraught with mixed emotions; however, it was clear to me that the Lord was calling me to start the next chapter and to expand my vision. Collectively, I had worked together with a highly talented team and we accomplished extraordinary results. When I looked back over the years, I continued to be amazed at the contributions of the team in building global leadership capability across the world. The Global Leadership Curriculum was award-winning, with programs such as the Senior Executive Forum, Executive Development Program, Managing Directors Forum, Leadership Excellence, Employee Engagement, and Leading Technical Professionals Program. The programs were designed to build leadership talent for GM to continue to win in the global marketplace. How could I possibly leave the company when there was more to accomplish?

In 2004, the college was given a challenge to build a global and common approach to developing newly appointed leaders. This task appeared to be mission impossible; however, with extraordinary colleagues from around the world – in all four regions – who were committed to learning as well as excellence, we made it happen. The Global Leadership Program was designed and developed over the course of four years. It launched in February of 2008, building global leadership talent around the world. This was a remarkable journey, which led to the culmination of the final GM chapter completed for the Global Leadership Curriculum. This mission was accomplished by an extraordinary global team.

The final GM chapter was bittersweet. I retired from the company with sadness in my heart, leaving a wonderful team and the marvelous work – a team and work that I thoroughly loved and enjoyed. While it was a tremendously difficult decision for me to make, in my heart, I know it was best. I knew that God was calling for me to expand my vision beyond the automotive industry. In departing, it left room for even greater accomplishments in building global capability and a time to refresh, renew, and to re-energize strategies related to leadership development. I was excited about the future and the opportunities that lie ahead; however, the future was unknown. While the path was not clear, I knew that the path was there, and I looked forward to the next journey with great expectation.

Looking to the future following retirement, my immediate plans included spending time with my family and friends, which had been hampered by extensive global travel. There were opportunities presented prior to departing from GM. It was clear that God was expanding my vision and creating yet another blessing zone prospect. The new prospect was the move to Phoenix, resulting from a job opportunity. While I thought I was relocating to Phoenix for another job, it turned out to be a profound opportunity to birth the ministry of Victorious Women. Truly, the Lord expanded my vision of possibilities. The calling was clear. The alone time in Phoenix led to a clear path of focus and purpose.

Mission Statement

The mission of **Victorious Women Ministries** is to touch the lives of women by the transforming power of Jesus Christ, encouraging them to follow His example and teaching them to discover their personal mission as revealed through their relationship with Christ.

Purpose

Victorious Women is a ministry committed to proclaiming God's Word without compromise, praising Him with reverence, and striving to become women of faith, unity, and praise. Our purpose is to a specific ministry focused on women as a component of their spiritual development. The purpose can only be accomplished through the power of the Holy Spirit.

Statement of Purpose

- **Service to Others:** A support system for women.
- **Evangelism:** Seeking venues to increase the fold for Christ. Women to follow Christ's example and live meaningful and victorious lives.
- **The Blessing Zone:** An atmosphere for women to deepen their walk with the Lord, develop their gifts and abilities, and enhance their relationship with the Lord.
- **Teaching:** Create venues for women to discover God's perfect plan for their lives and to honor Him in every facet of their lives.
- **Leadership:** Developing capability to lead in areas of giftedness.

Scriptural Foundation

"Finally, my brethren, be strong in the Lord and in the power of His might." (Ephesians 6:10 NKJV)

Goal

The goal is to be the premier source of support for women in need of a closer walk with the Lord. This is accomplished through consistent alignment with the mission of Victorious Women and to the statement of purpose. Additionally, the goal is to assist women of all ages to become Godly women who serve the Lord our God, our families, as well as the community of which we are a part of with **excellence.**

Motto

A Higher Calling: Victorious Women in Christ!

Look forward to the future – the prize is in front of you – your calling awaits! Embrace your blessing zone with passion and purpose.

Chapter 7: Expand Your Vision to See Your Blessing Zone

Notes

Appendix

THE BLESSING ZONE
Study Guide

Chapter 1: Study Guide

Discover Your Blessing Zone

Discussion and Reflection

1. **Enrich your life.** How can you enrich your life to experience your unique blessing zone?

_____
_____
_____
_____
_____
_____
_____
_____
_____
_____

2. **Explore God's plan.** How can you grow to value God's plan for you?

3. **Engage with God.** What is one action you can take to engage with God?

Chapter 1: Study Guide
Discover Your Blessing Zone
Notes

THE BLESSING ZONE

Chapter 2: Study Guide
Enrich Your Life
Discussion and Reflection

1. How have you been stirred by the Holy Spirit in the past?

___
___
___
___
___
___
___
___
___
___

2. What actions did you take?

3. What learning have you discovered during a lonely period of your life?

Chapter 2: Study Guide

Enrich Your Life

Notes

THE BLESSING ZONE

Chapter 3: Study Guide

Explore God's Plan

Discussion and Reflection

1. Live every day with courage, joy, and peace. What action can you take to live life with courage?

_____
_____
_____
_____
_____
_____
_____
_____
_____

2. See obstacles as opportunities to show God's mercy and grace. How has God demonstrated His mercy and grace to you? Provide one example.

3. Give to others and see giving as an opening to plant seeds of hope. How might your giving change based on Maria's story?

Chapter 3: Study Guide

Explore God's Plan

Notes

THE BLESSING ZONE

Chapter 4: Study Guide
Engage with God

Discussion and Reflection

1. God is always there, waiting for us to draw nearer. Why is it challenging to draw near to God? Provide one example.

___
___
___
___
___
___
___
___

2. Times of loneliness create superb opportunities to engage with God if we open our hearts to Him. How can you use loneliness to engage with God?

3. Seize opportunities to engage with God -- not just when all is well. Sometimes, the best opportunities emerge during times of trial. What is a barrier that gets in the way of engaging with God? Provide one example.

Chapter 4: Study Guide
Engage with God
Notes

Chapter 5: Study Guide

Experience the Richness of The Blessing Zone

Discussion and Reflection

1. How does your life honor God?

_____

_____

_____

_____

_____

_____

_____

_____

_____

2. How have you allowed God to use you to bring Him glory? Provide one example.

3. What has God shown you about yourself that provides direction in understanding His plan for you?

Chapter 5: Experience the Richness of The Blessing Zone

Notes

Chapter 6: Study Guide

Enhance Your Relationship with Him

Discussion and Reflection

1. What has God spoken to your heart when experiencing a new adventure?

___
___
___
___
___
___
___
___
___

2. Why are new adventures important in building faith?

3. How can you open your heart to new adventures?

Chapter 6: Study Guide
Enhance Your Relationship with Him
Notes

Chapter 7: Study Guide
Expand Your Vision to See Your Blessing Zone
Discussion and Reflection

1. What is your mission statement?

2. What is your purpose statement?

3. How can you expand your vision to experience your blessing zone?

Chapter 7: Study Guide
Expand Your Vision to See Your Blessing Zone

Notes

THE BLESSING ZONE

Chapter 1: Discover Your Blessing Zone!

Points to Remember

- **Enrich your life.** Acknowledge that the blessing zone is a real place.
- **Explore God's plan.** Appreciate the Master's plan for you.
- **Engage with God.** Align yourself with His love letter to you – the Bible.
- **Experience the richness of the blessing zone.** Attend to God's presence. He is always there.
- **Enhance your relationship with Him.** Accept His goodness and, in times of trial and tribulation, you will be glad you did.

- **Expand your vision to see your blessing zone.** Apply what is needed from your journey to create your divinely inspired vision of your blessing zone.

THE BLESSING ZONE

Chapter 2: Enrich Your Life
Point to Remember

Acknowledge:
The Blessing Zone is a real place.

THE BLESSING ZONE

Chapter 3: Explore God's Plan

Points to Remember

- Live every day with courage, joy, and peace.
- See obstacles as opportunities to show God's mercy and grace.
- Give to others and see giving as an opening to plant seeds of hope.
- Recognize the power of relationships, with God and with others.
- Embrace the love that only comes from God.
- Stay the course. Keep it moving!
- Appreciate the Master's plan and endure the race set before you.

THE BLESSING ZONE

Chapter 4: Engage with God
Points to Remember

- God is always there, waiting for us to draw nearer.
- Times of loneliness create superb opportunities to engage with God if we open our hearts to Him.
- Seize opportunities to engage with God – not just when all is well. Sometimes, the best opportunities emerge during times of trial.
- Seek clarity of God's plans, purpose, and passion that He designed specifically for you.
- Trust God always as His path for you unfolds.

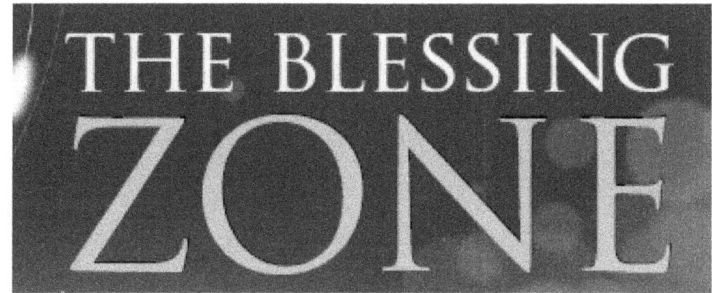

Chapter 5: Experience the Richness Of the Blessing Zone

Points to Remember

Focused Prayer: Be Specific

- God's plan to unfold in a way that brings Him honor and for His will be done.
- Pray for specific outcomes – that the Lord provides His wisdom, strength, courage, and power to unleash everything He has for us.
- To pray for the team – that all planning goes extremely well.
- To pray for an experience without barriers.
- To pray for excellent health and direction for all who are involved.

Chapter 6: Enhance Your Relationship with Him

Points to Remember

Key Scripture: John 3:16 NKJV: *For God so loved the world that He gave His only begotten Son, that whoever believes in Him should not perish but have everlasting life.*

- Build your relationship with God through trials and tribulations.

Chapter 7: Expand Your Vision To See Your Blessing Zone

Points to Remember

- Align with God.
- Clarify your vision.
- Understand your mission.
- Understand your purpose.
- Create your goals and plans.
- Experience the richness of "The Blessing Zone" by serving others!

www.ingramcontent.com/pod-product-compliance
Lightning Source LLC
Chambersburg PA
CBHW071129090426
42736CB00012B/2064